A Numerology Series

by

Lloyd Leon

THREE

Life Path Three

Contents

Chapter 1

Understanding Life Path 3

The Essence of Life Path 3

The essence of Life Path 3 is fundamentally rooted in creativity, self-expression, and joy. Individuals on this path are often characterized by their artistic flair and a natural inclination toward communication. They possess an innate ability to inspire others through their vibrant personalities and imaginative ideas. This subchapter delves into the core attributes of Life Path 3, emphasizing how these qualities not only define their identity but also serve as powerful catalysts for personal and communal growth. By embracing their creative spirit, Life Path 3 individuals can unlock their true potential and navigate the complexities of life with grace and enthusiasm.

Creativity is the lifeblood of Life Path 3. Those who embody this path are often drawn to various forms of artistic expression, whether it be writing, painting, music, or performance. This creative energy is not merely a hobby; it is a fundamental aspect of their identity that fuels their passion and purpose. Engaging in artistic endeavors allows Life Path 3 individuals to communicate their thoughts and emotions effectively, bridging the gap between themselves and the world around them. By nurturing this creative spirit, they can enhance their confidence and overcome self-doubt, transforming their vulnerabilities into strengths.

Communication skills are another hallmark of Life Path 3 individuals. Their ability to articulate ideas and connect with others is often exceptional, enabling them to form meaningful relationships. However, effective communication also requires active listening and empathy, which are essential for building community and nurturing relationships. As Life Path 3 individuals develop these skills, they create spaces where collaboration and shared experiences thrive. This not only enriches their social life but also fosters personal growth, as they learn from diverse perspectives and experiences.

Balancing the social aspects of life with personal development is crucial for those on Life Path 3. While they naturally gravitate towards social interactions, it is essential to carve out time for introspection and mindfulness practices. These practices help enhance emotional well-being, allowing them to process their feelings and cultivate a positive mindset. By integrating mindfulness into their daily routines, Life Path 3 individuals can navigate challenges with resilience and maintain a joyful outlook. This balance between social engagement and personal reflection is key to achieving their dreams and finding deeper fulfillment.

In terms of career paths, Life Path 3 individuals often thrive in environments that allow for creativity and interpersonal connection. Fields such as art, writing, performing, and teaching provide ample opportunities for self-expression and collaboration. By setting clear goals and pursuing their passions with determination, they can achieve their dreams while contributing positively to their communities. Additionally, nurturing relationships within their professional circles can lead to collaborative projects that further enhance their creativity and joy. Ultimately, embracing the essence of Life Path 3 paves the way for a fulfilling life filled with purpose, connection, and creative expression.

Characteristics and Traits

Individuals on the Life Path 3 journey possess a unique set of characteristics and traits that make them particularly adept at navigating the complexities of creative expression and interpersonal communication. At the core, Life Path 3 individuals are often characterized by their vibrant energy and enthusiasm for life. This innate zest fuels their creative endeavors, allowing them to approach artistic projects with an open heart and an imaginative mind. They tend to exude charisma, drawing others to their vibrant personality, which often results in an expansive social network. This ability to connect with others not only enriches their personal lives but also enhances their creative output, as collaboration often leads to new ideas and inspiration.

Creativity and self-expression stand out as defining traits for those on Life Path 3. These individuals often thrive in artistic environments, whether through writing, visual arts, or performing. Their imaginative capabilities allow them to think outside the box, producing original work that resonates with a wide audience. However, this creative spirit can sometimes be accompanied by a tendency towards self-doubt, particularly when they compare themselves to others or face criticism. Recognizing this vulnerability is essential for Life Path 3 individuals, as it opens the door to overcoming obstacles and building confidence in their abilities. Learning to embrace their unique style and voice is crucial in fostering a strong sense of self-worth.

Communication skills are another hallmark of Life Path 3 individuals. They are often natural storytellers, able to articulate their thoughts and emotions with clarity and flair. This talent not only enhances their creative projects but also plays a vital role in personal and professional relationships. Developing these communication skills further can lead to improved connections with others, allowing Life Path 3 individuals to express their needs and desires more effectively. Engaging in active listening and empathetic dialogue can strengthen their relationships, offering support and understanding in both personal and communal settings.

As Life Path 3 individuals navigate the balance between their social lives and personal growth, they may find themselves needing to set boundaries to protect their creative energy. While their sociable nature draws them into numerous activities, it is essential that they carve out time for introspection and self-care. Mindfulness practices can be beneficial in maintaining emotional well-being, helping them to cultivate joy and positivity in their lives. By integrating techniques such as meditation, journaling, and creative visualization into their routines, Life Path 3 individuals can enhance their emotional resilience and clarify their goals.

Ultimately, individuals on Life Path 3 are called to embrace their authentic selves while nurturing their relationships with others. By recognizing their unique characteristics and traits, they can unlock their true potential and achieve their dreams. Whether through pursuing creative careers, fostering community connections, or embarking on spiritual growth, Life Path 3 individuals have the innate ability to inspire both themselves and those around them. Emphasizing self-acceptance and continuous growth can lead them to a fulfilling and purpose-driven life.

The Creative Spirit of Life Path 3

The Creative Spirit of Life Path 3 embodies a vibrant energy that thrives on self-expression and artistic exploration. Individuals on this path are often characterized by their innate ability to communicate ideas and emotions through various creative outlets. Whether it is through writing, visual arts, music, or performing, the essence of Life Path 3 lies in the transformative power of creativity. This subchapter delves into the unique attributes of Life Path 3, highlighting how these individuals can harness their creative spirit to unlock their true potential and achieve personal fulfillment.

At the heart of Life Path 3 is the desire for self-expression. Those who resonate with this path often find themselves drawn to the arts, using creativity as a means to convey their thoughts and feelings. Developing communication skills is crucial for Life Path 3 individuals, as it enhances their ability to connect with others and share their artistic vision. Engaging in creative practices not only serves as a form of personal expression but also fosters a deeper understanding of oneself, paving the way for emotional growth and resilience. By embracing their creative spirit, Life Path 3 individuals can effectively navigate their emotions and develop a more profound sense of self-awareness.

However, the journey of a Life Path 3 individual is not without its challenges. Overcoming self-doubt and building confidence are essential components of nurturing the creative spirit. It is common for those on this path to grapple with insecurities, often questioning their talents and worth. To counteract this, cultivating a positive mindset and surrounding oneself with supportive communities can significantly enhance confidence levels. Embracing failure as a part of the creative process rather than a setback allows Life Path 3 individuals to flourish in their pursuits, ultimately leading to greater artistic freedom and innovation.

Balancing social life and personal growth is another critical aspect of Life Path 3. Individuals on this journey thrive in social settings, often drawing inspiration and energy from their interactions with others. However, it is essential for them to carve out time for introspection and personal development. Mindfulness practices can play a vital role in achieving this balance, enabling Life Path 3 individuals to cultivate emotional well-being while also nurturing their creative pursuits. Engaging in activities such as meditation, journaling, or nature walks can enhance their ability to connect with their inner selves, fostering a sense of joy and positivity that fuels their creative expression.

In conclusion, the creative spirit of Life Path 3 is a powerful force that can lead to profound personal and spiritual growth. By embracing their unique talents, developing communication skills, and fostering supportive relationships, individuals can unlock their true potential. Career opportunities abound for those on this path, particularly in fields that allow for creative expression and collaboration. By setting clear goals and maintaining a positive mindset, Life Path 3 individuals can achieve their dreams and contribute to their communities. Ultimately, nurturing the creative spirit not only enriches their lives but also inspires others on their journeys, creating a ripple effect of creativity and positivity in the world.

Chapter 2

Unlocking Your True Life Potential

Identifying Your Unique Gifts

Identifying your unique gifts is a crucial step on the journey of a Life Path 3 individual. Life Path 3 is often associated with creativity, self-expression, and communication. To fully embrace these attributes, it is essential to recognize what sets you apart from others. This process begins with introspection and a willingness to explore your passions, interests, and talents. Reflecting on moments when you felt most alive and engaged can provide insights into your innate abilities. Consider your hobbies, the activities that bring you joy, and the skills that come naturally to you. Journaling these experiences can help clarify the gifts that resonate with your true self.

Another approach to identifying your unique gifts is through feedback from those around you. Friends, family, and mentors can offer valuable perspectives on your strengths and talents that you may not see in yourself. Engaging in open conversations about your skills can shine a light on aspects of your personality that contribute to your creative spirit. Additionally, consider participating in group activities or workshops that encourage collaboration and creativity. These environments can provide opportunities to showcase your abilities and receive constructive feedback, further enhancing your self-awareness.

Exploring various forms of artistic expression is also a powerful way to identify your unique gifts. Life Path 3 individuals often thrive in creative fields, and experimenting with different mediums can reveal hidden talents. Whether it's painting, writing, music, or performance, allowing yourself the freedom to explore can lead to unexpected discoveries about your capabilities. Keep in mind that embracing vulnerability in your creative pursuits can unlock your potential. As you try new things, notice which activities spark joy and fulfillment, as these may indicate your unique gifts waiting to be nurtured.

Moreover, identifying your unique gifts involves recognizing the qualities that enhance your communication skills. Life Path 3 individuals are often natural communicators, but understanding how you convey your thoughts and emotions can refine your abilities. Pay attention to how you connect with others, whether through storytelling, humor, or empathy. Cultivating these aspects can help you articulate your ideas more effectively, allowing your unique gifts to shine through in your interactions. Consider practicing active listening and engaging in conversations that challenge you, as these experiences can broaden your communication repertoire.

Lastly, overcoming self-doubt is integral in the process of identifying and embracing your unique gifts. Life Path 3 individuals may struggle with confidence, often questioning their creative abilities. It is essential to recognize that self-doubt is a common experience and can be transformed into motivation for growth. Establishing a supportive network of like-minded individuals can provide encouragement and inspiration as you navigate this journey. Setting small, achievable goals related to your creative pursuits can gradually build your confidence, allowing you to fully express your unique gifts and contribute to the world around you.

Embracing Change and Growth

Embracing change and growth is an essential aspect of the journey for individuals on Life Path 3. This path, characterized by creativity, self-expression, and communication, inherently invites transformation. By recognizing that change is a natural part of life, those on this path can cultivate a mindset that not only accepts but also celebrates the evolution of their creative spirit. This journey is about more than just artistic expression; it involves a holistic approach to personal development, intertwining emotional well-being, social interactions, and spiritual growth.

To fully embrace change, Life Path 3 individuals must first acknowledge their own creative potential. This recognition is crucial for overcoming self-doubt, a common challenge for those who are sensitive and expressive. By engaging in activities that foster creativity—be it through writing, painting, or performing—individuals can build confidence in their abilities. This practice not only enhances their artistic skills but also serves as a vehicle for personal growth. Through the act of creation, they learn to navigate the uncertainties of life, transforming challenges into opportunities for innovation and self-discovery.

Communication is another vital component of embracing change for Life Path 3 individuals. Effective communication skills enable them to express their thoughts and feelings clearly, fostering deeper connections with others. These connections are essential for building a supportive community that can help navigate the complexities of change. By sharing their experiences and insights, they contribute to a collective understanding of growth, allowing both themselves and others to flourish. This network of relationships can provide encouragement and inspiration, reinforcing the idea that change can be met with positivity and resilience.

Mindfulness practices can significantly enhance the ability to embrace change and growth. By incorporating techniques such as meditation, journaling, or mindful breathing, individuals can cultivate a greater awareness of their emotions and thoughts. This awareness is crucial when facing transitions, as it allows for a more grounded response to challenges. Life Path 3 individuals, often prone to emotional highs and lows, can benefit from these practices by fostering emotional stability and a more balanced perspective. This balance is essential for maintaining joy and positivity, even amidst the inevitable ups and downs of life.

Ultimately, embracing change and growth is about aligning with one's true potential and purpose. For Life Path 3 individuals, this alignment often manifests through creative expression and meaningful relationships. Setting clear goals and pursuing dreams becomes a pathway for not only personal fulfillment but also for contributing to the broader community. By embracing the fluid nature of life, they can navigate their unique journey with confidence and joy, transforming each change into a stepping stone towards greater creativity and fulfillment. In this way, Life Path 3 individuals can not only unlock their true potential but also inspire others to embark on their own journeys of growth and self-discovery.

Setting Intentions for Success

Setting intentions is a powerful practice that can significantly influence the trajectory of a Life Path 3 individual. The essence of Life Path 3 is rooted in creative expression and communication, which offers a unique opportunity to harness the energy of intentions for success. By clearly defining what success looks like for them, individuals on this path can align their creative pursuits with their deeper desires, allowing their artistic talents to flourish. Intentions act as guiding stars, providing clarity and direction amid the distractions of daily life.

To set effective intentions, it is essential for Life Path 3 individuals to engage in self-reflection. This process involves contemplating personal aspirations, strengths, and areas for growth. By examining their creative goals and the underlying motivations for these ambitions, they can articulate intentions that resonate deeply with their spirit. This introspective practice not only fosters creativity but also helps individuals combat self-doubt, laying the groundwork for building confidence in their artistic endeavors and communication skills.

Once intentions are established, the next step is to incorporate them into daily routines. Visualization techniques can be particularly beneficial for Life Path 3 individuals, as they naturally resonate with artistic visualization. Creating vision boards or practicing guided imagery can reinforce intentions, making them more tangible and achievable. Additionally, maintaining a journal where intentions are written down and regularly revisited can serve as a powerful reminder of their goals and aspirations, thus strengthening their commitment to personal growth and creative expression.

It is also crucial for Life Path 3 individuals to share their intentions with their community. By articulating their goals and aspirations to trusted friends or creative peers, they not only invite accountability but also create a supportive network that nurtures their journey. This practice enhances social connections, balancing personal growth with meaningful relationships. Engaging in dialogues about intentions and achievements can foster a sense of belonging, encouraging collaboration and collective creativity within their community.

Finally, embracing mindfulness practices can further enhance the effectiveness of setting intentions. Life Path 3 individuals can benefit from techniques such as meditation, deep breathing, and mindful observation to cultivate emotional well-being. These practices enable them to remain present, reducing anxiety and allowing for a more profound connection to their creative spirit. By grounding themselves in the moment, they can focus on their intentions with clarity and positivity, ultimately paving the way for success in their artistic and personal lives.

Chapter 3

Creative Expression and Artistry

Exploring Different Art Forms

Art serves as a powerful medium for self-expression and connection, especially for individuals on the Life Path 3 journey. This path emphasizes creativity, communication, and social interaction, making it essential to explore various art forms that resonate with one's unique spirit. By engaging with different artistic modalities, individuals can tap into their inherent creativity, enhancing their ability to express thoughts and feelings while fostering deeper connections with others. Whether through visual arts, performing arts, or literary pursuits, each form offers unique opportunities for personal growth and emotional exploration.

Visual arts encompass a broad range of practices, including painting, sculpture, photography, and digital media. For Life Path 3 individuals, these mediums provide a canvas for their vibrant emotions and imaginative ideas. Engaging in visual arts allows for experimentation with colors, shapes, and textures, leading to a deeper understanding of one's emotional landscape. This exploration not only cultivates technical skills but also promotes mindfulness, as the artist becomes immersed in the creative process. Such experiences can help Life Path 3 individuals overcome self-doubt, transforming vulnerability into powerful works of art that reflect their inner truths.

The performing arts, including theater, dance, and music, also hold significant potential for Life Path 3 individuals. These dynamic forms of expression encourage collaboration and communication, essential traits for those on this life path. Participating in group performances fosters a sense of community and belonging, as artists share their stories and emotions with an audience. This connection can be particularly uplifting, instilling a sense of joy and positivity. Additionally, performing arts provide a platform for individuals to confront and transcend personal challenges, ultimately leading to greater confidence and self-assuredness.

Literary arts, such as poetry, storytelling, and creative writing, offer another avenue for exploration. Writing allows Life Path 3 individuals to articulate their thoughts and feelings in a structured manner, helping them develop their communication skills. Through the written word, they can navigate complex emotions, confront self-doubt, and articulate their dreams and aspirations. The act of writing can be both cathartic and empowering, nurturing emotional well-being and encouraging personal reflection. By sharing their stories, individuals not only connect with others but also contribute to a larger narrative that fosters understanding and empathy within their communities.

Ultimately, exploring different art forms is a vital aspect of nurturing the creative spirit inherent in Life Path 3 individuals. Each artistic modality offers distinct benefits, from enhancing emotional expression and building confidence to fostering social connections and personal growth. By embracing a diverse range of creative practices, individuals can unlock their true potential, cultivate joy, and find purpose in their artistic endeavors. This journey of exploration not only enriches their lives but also inspires those around them, creating a ripple effect that fosters a deeper appreciation for the power of creativity in the world.

Finding Your Creative Voice

Finding your creative voice is a transformative journey, particularly for those on the Life Path 3. As a Life Path 3 individual, you are naturally inclined towards creative expression, artistry, and communication. However, this intuitive gift can sometimes be clouded by self-doubt or external expectations. To truly unlock your potential, it is essential to embark on a quest to discover and cultivate your unique voice. This process involves introspection, experimentation, and the willingness to embrace vulnerability.

The first step in finding your creative voice is self-reflection. Take time to explore your passions, interests, and experiences that resonate with you. Journaling can be an invaluable tool in this phase. Write freely about what moves you, what inspires you, and what you wish to communicate to the world. This practice helps clarify your thoughts and feelings, allowing you to identify recurring themes that can guide your creative expression. Pay attention to the moments when you feel most alive and engaged; these are often key indicators of your authentic voice.

Experimentation is equally important in the journey of self-discovery. Allow yourself to try different mediums and forms of expression without the pressure of perfection. Whether it's painting, writing, dancing, or any other art form, give yourself permission to play and explore. This exploratory phase can lead to unexpected breakthroughs, helping you uncover aspects of your creativity that you may not have recognized before. Embrace mistakes as part of the process; they often lead to valuable insights and innovations that can shape your voice.

Building confidence is another crucial aspect of finding your creative voice. Life Path 3 individuals often grapple with self-doubt, which can stifle creativity. To counter this, practice affirmations and surround yourself with supportive people who uplift and encourage you. Share your work with trusted friends or join creative groups where you can receive constructive feedback. Engaging with others not only enhances your skills but also fosters a sense of community that nurtures your growth. Remember, every artist has faced challenges; your journey is uniquely yours, and embracing it will strengthen your self-belief.

Finally, integrating mindfulness into your daily routine can significantly enhance your creative process. Mindfulness practices, such as meditation or deep breathing, help cultivate emotional well-being and clarity of thought. By grounding yourself in the present moment, you can quiet the noise of self-doubt and external distractions, allowing your true voice to emerge. Set aside dedicated time for creative endeavors, and approach them with an open heart and mind. This intentionality not only enriches your creative output but also aligns your artistry with your life's purpose, ultimately leading to a more fulfilling and joyful existence.

Overcoming Creative Blocks

Creative blocks are a common challenge faced by individuals on Life Path 3, known for their expressive and artistic nature. Understanding the roots of these blocks is essential for unlocking one's true life potential. Often, creative blocks arise from self-doubt, fear of judgment, or an overwhelming desire for perfection. Recognizing these emotional barriers can be the first step toward overcoming them. Embracing the Life Path 3's innate creativity involves acknowledging these feelings as part of the journey, rather than as insurmountable obstacles.

One effective technique for overcoming creative blocks is to engage in mindfulness practices. Mindfulness encourages individuals to be present in the moment, allowing thoughts and feelings to flow freely without judgment. By incorporating mindfulness exercises into daily routines, Life Path 3 individuals can cultivate a more relaxed mental state, reducing anxiety that often accompanies creative endeavors. Simple practices such as deep breathing or meditation can create a safe space for ideas to emerge without the pressure of immediate productivity.

Another useful strategy involves the concept of playfulness in creative expression. Life Path 3 individuals are naturally inclined toward joy and spontaneity, so tapping into these traits can help to break the cycle of rigidity that often accompanies creative blocks. Engaging in activities that are purely for fun, such as doodling, improvisational theater, or even playful brainstorming sessions, can reignite the creative spark. By shifting the focus from outcomes to the sheer joy of creation, individuals can often find new pathways for inspiration.

Collaboration is another powerful tool for overcoming creative blocks. Life Path 3 individuals thrive in social settings, making collaboration an ideal way to reignite creativity. Working with others can provide fresh perspectives and ideas, helping to dissolve the isolation that often accompanies creative struggles. Whether through group art projects, writing workshops, or simply sharing thoughts with friends, the energy and enthusiasm of collaborative efforts can serve as a catalyst for overcoming blocks.

Lastly, setting realistic goals can significantly aid in overcoming creative blocks. Life Path 3 individuals may set high expectations for themselves, leading to feelings of inadequacy when those expectations are not met. By breaking down larger creative projects into smaller, manageable tasks, individuals can create a sense of accomplishment and motivation. Celebrating small victories fosters confidence and encourages continued exploration of creative pursuits. This approach not only alleviates pressure but also nurtures the playful and expressive spirit inherent in Life Path 3 individuals.

Chapter 4

Developing Communication Skills

The Power of Words

Words possess an extraordinary power that extends far beyond mere communication. For individuals on Life Path 3, which emphasizes creativity, self-expression, and social interaction, words can become a potent tool for unlocking inner potential. This life path encourages the exploration of artistic talents and creativity, channeling personal experiences and emotions into expressions that resonate with others. By mastering the art of language, those on Life Path 3 can convey their ideas, evoke emotions, and inspire change, both within themselves and in the lives of others.

Effective communication is a cornerstone for personal and professional success, particularly for individuals who thrive on social connections. Life Path 3 individuals often excel in expressing themselves artistically, yet the ability to articulate thoughts and feelings verbally is equally important. Developing communication skills can enhance relationships, foster collaboration, and create opportunities for growth. By choosing words wisely and expressing themselves clearly, Life Path 3s can connect with others on a deeper level, facilitating understanding and building a supportive community.

Overcoming self-doubt is a common challenge for those on Life Path 3, and words play a crucial role in this journey. The narratives we tell ourselves influence our self-perception and confidence levels. By consciously choosing empowering language, individuals can transform negative self-talk into affirmations that promote positivity and resilience. This shift in mindset not only builds self-esteem but also encourages the pursuit of creative endeavors without fear of judgment. Embracing the power of words can lead to profound personal growth and a renewed sense of purpose.

Joy and positivity are essential components of a fulfilling life, and language can amplify these qualities. Life Path 3 individuals can harness the power of words to cultivate an optimistic outlook, both for themselves and their communities. Sharing uplifting stories, expressing gratitude, and engaging in positive affirmations can create an atmosphere of encouragement and support. By fostering a culture of positivity through their words, Life Path 3s can inspire others to embrace their own creative journeys, ultimately contributing to a more vibrant and connected society.

As individuals on Life Path 3 navigate their unique paths, the intentional use of words can significantly impact their spiritual growth and personal development. By setting goals and articulating their dreams, they can manifest their desires into reality. Mindfulness practices that incorporate verbal affirmations and reflective journaling can enhance emotional well-being, guiding them toward clarity and purpose. Ultimately, the power of words serves as a vital resource, enabling those on Life Path 3 to not only express their creativity but also to uplift themselves and others in the pursuit of their highest potential.

Effective Listening Techniques

Effective listening techniques are essential for individuals on Life Path 3, as they foster authentic connections and enhance creative expression. Engaging fully with others not only enriches personal relationships but also stimulates inspiration for artistic endeavors. To become an effective listener, one must cultivate an environment of openness and receptivity. This involves setting aside distractions, both external and internal, and being fully present in the moment. Practicing mindfulness can aid in this process, allowing the listener to focus on the speaker without preconceived notions or judgments.

Active listening is a vital technique that can significantly improve communication skills for those on Life Path 3. This method involves not only hearing the words being spoken but also understanding the emotions and intentions behind them. To practice active listening, individuals should employ techniques such as nodding, maintaining eye contact, and summarizing what the speaker has conveyed. These actions demonstrate genuine interest and help clarify any misunderstandings, ultimately leading to more meaningful interactions. Engaging in this practice not only enhances interpersonal relationships but also bolsters self-confidence by validating one's ability to connect with others.

Empathetic listening is another crucial technique that can help Life Path 3 individuals navigate their social landscapes while balancing personal growth. This approach requires the listener to put themselves in the speaker's shoes, striving to understand their perspective and feelings. By doing so, listeners can create a safe space for open dialogue, which is particularly important for nurturing relationships and building community. Empathetic listening encourages vulnerability, allowing individuals to share their thoughts and emotions freely, ultimately fostering deeper connections that can lead to collaborative artistic ventures.

In addition to these techniques, maintaining a positive mindset while listening can significantly impact the quality of interactions. Life Path 3 individuals are often characterized by their joyful and optimistic nature, which can be a powerful tool when engaging with others. Approaching conversations with positivity allows listeners to remain open to new ideas and perspectives, enhancing their creative output. Furthermore, a positive attitude can help mitigate feelings of self-doubt, reinforcing confidence in one's abilities to communicate effectively and connect with others.

Finally, incorporating reflective listening can further enhance the listening experience for Life Path 3 individuals. This technique involves not only understanding and empathizing with the speaker but also reflecting on the conversation afterward to glean insights and lessons. Taking time to process what has been discussed can lead to personal growth and deeper self-awareness, which are essential components of the Life Path 3 journey. By continually refining listening skills through these techniques, individuals can unlock their true potential, enrich their creative expressions, and cultivate meaningful relationships that support their artistic endeavors.

Building Rapport and Connection

Building rapport and connection is a fundamental aspect of personal and professional growth for individuals on Life Path 3. This life path, characterized by creativity, self-expression, and communication, thrives on the ability to forge meaningful relationships. Establishing connections with others not only enriches your social life but also enhances your creative expression. For numerologers, understanding the dynamics of rapport can be the key to unlocking the true potential of those on this path, fostering an environment where creativity can flourish.

To build rapport, one must first develop strong communication skills. Effective communication goes beyond mere words; it involves active listening, empathy, and the ability to read non-verbal cues. Individuals on Life Path 3 often possess an innate charm and charisma, making it easier for them to engage with others. However, honing these skills can elevate their interactions to a deeper level. Practicing active listening allows them to connect with others genuinely, ensuring that conversations are not just exchanges but opportunities for mutual understanding and growth.

Overcoming self-doubt is another critical component of building connections. Life Path 3 individuals may struggle with insecurity, impacting their ability to relate to others. By cultivating self-confidence, they can present their authentic selves, attracting like-minded individuals and fostering stronger relationships. Techniques such as positive affirmations and visualization can aid in overcoming these barriers, allowing for a more genuine connection with others. As self-doubt diminishes, the ability to engage openly and honestly increases, creating a solid foundation for rapport.

Balancing social life and personal growth is essential for individuals on this path. While it is vital to nurture relationships, it is equally important to dedicate time to self-reflection and personal development. Mindfulness practices can enhance emotional well-being, allowing individuals to become more present in their interactions. By integrating mindfulness into their daily routines, Life Path 3 individuals can cultivate a deeper sense of awareness, both of themselves and of the connections they are building. This balance fosters joy and positivity, which are infectious and can significantly enhance social dynamics.

Ultimately, nurturing relationships and building community are integral to the Life Path 3 experience. Connections formed through shared interests, values, and experiences can lead to collaborative opportunities and creative partnerships. Setting goals for social engagement, such as joining groups or participating in community events, can help individuals on this path expand their networks. By actively seeking to connect with others, they not only enrich their own lives but also contribute positively to the lives of those around them, reinforcing the importance of community in the journey of personal and creative development.

Chapter 5

Overcoming Self-Doubt and Building Confidence

Understanding Self-Doubt

Self-doubt is a common experience that can significantly impact the creative expression and overall well-being of individuals on Life Path 3. This path is often associated with creativity, communication, and social interaction, making self-doubt particularly challenging for those who thrive on self-expression. Understanding the roots of self-doubt is essential for Life Path 3 individuals, as it can inhibit the vibrant energy needed to fulfill their creative potential. This subchapter will explore the nature of self-doubt, its effects on creativity, and strategies for overcoming it.

At its core, self-doubt is an internal dialogue that questions one's abilities and worth. For those on Life Path 3, this can manifest as feelings of inadequacy in their artistic endeavors or communication skills. The fear of not being good enough can prevent individuals from sharing their work or expressing their ideas, which is counterproductive to their innate talents. Recognizing this pattern is the first step in dismantling the inner critic that fuels self-doubt. By acknowledging the presence of self-doubt, individuals can begin to separate their true potential from the limiting beliefs that hold them back.

The impact of self-doubt can extend beyond personal creativity and communication. It can seep into social interactions, leading to a reluctance to engage or participate in collaborative projects. Life Path 3 individuals often thrive in vibrant social environments, yet self-doubt can create barriers that hinder connection with others. This can foster isolation and negatively affect emotional well-being. Understanding the interplay between self-doubt and social engagement is crucial for Life Path 3 individuals, as it highlights the importance of nurturing both creative and interpersonal skills to maintain a balanced life.

To combat self-doubt, individuals on Life Path 3 can employ several techniques aimed at building confidence and resilience. One effective strategy is the practice of positive affirmations, which can help reframe negative thoughts and reinforce self-worth. Additionally, setting achievable goals can provide a clear pathway to success, allowing individuals to celebrate small victories that bolster their confidence. Engaging in mindfulness practices can also aid in grounding one's thoughts and emotions, creating a space for self-acceptance and clarity. Embracing a growth mindset further empowers Life Path 3 individuals to view challenges as opportunities for learning rather than as threats to their self-esteem.

Ultimately, overcoming self-doubt is a journey that requires patience and self-compassion. Life Path 3 individuals should remember that their creative spirit is a unique gift that deserves to be shared with the world. By understanding the nature of self-doubt and employing effective strategies to combat it, they can unlock their true potential, enhance their communication skills, and foster meaningful relationships. Embracing creativity with confidence not only enriches their own lives but also inspires those around them, creating a ripple effect of positivity and connection in their communities.

Strategies for Building Confidence

Building confidence is a crucial endeavor for individuals on Life Path 3, as it directly influences creative expression and personal growth. One effective strategy for enhancing confidence is to engage in regular self-reflection. By setting aside time to assess one's accomplishments, strengths, and areas for improvement, individuals can develop a clearer understanding of their unique talents. This practice not only reinforces a sense of self-worth but also creates a foundation for setting realistic goals, which can lead to further achievements and bolster confidence.

Another powerful approach to building confidence is through the cultivation of a supportive community. Life Path 3 individuals thrive in social settings, and surrounding oneself with positive, encouraging people can significantly impact self-esteem. Participating in groups that share similar interests, such as art, communication, or personal development, fosters an environment where creative expression is celebrated. Engaging in discussions, sharing experiences, and receiving constructive feedback can help individuals recognize their value and capabilities, thereby enhancing their confidence.

Practicing mindfulness is another essential strategy for building confidence. Mindfulness techniques, such as meditation and deep breathing exercises, can help individuals manage anxiety and self-doubt. By focusing on the present moment, individuals can reduce negative self-talk and cultivate a more positive self-image. Regular mindfulness practice can lead to a greater sense of emotional well-being, allowing Life Path 3 individuals to approach challenges with a more resilient mindset and increased confidence.

Setting small, achievable goals is also an effective method for building confidence incrementally. Life Path 3 individuals are naturally creative and expressive, but they may struggle with self-doubt when faced with larger aspirations. By breaking down larger goals into smaller, manageable steps, individuals can experience a series of successes that reinforce their belief in their abilities. Celebrating these small victories not only boosts confidence but also encourages continued growth and exploration in various aspects of life.

Lastly, embracing vulnerability can be a transformative strategy for building confidence. Life Path 3 individuals often fear judgment, which can stifle their creative expression. By allowing themselves to be vulnerable, whether through sharing personal stories or showcasing their art, they can connect with others on a deeper level. This openness fosters authenticity and encourages reciprocation, leading to stronger relationships and a greater sense of belonging. Ultimately, by embracing vulnerability, individuals can dismantle the barriers of self-doubt and cultivate a more profound confidence in their creative journeys.

Celebrating Your Achievements

Celebrating your achievements is a vital aspect of personal growth and creative expression, particularly for those on the Life Path 3 journey. Life Path 3 individuals are naturally inclined towards creativity, communication, and social engagement, making it essential to recognize and honor their accomplishments. Each success, no matter how small, serves as a building block for greater confidence and motivation. By taking the time to celebrate these moments, you reinforce your creative spirit and acknowledge the progress you've made, fostering a positive mindset that propels you forward.

One effective way to celebrate achievements is through reflective journaling. This practice allows Life Path 3 individuals to articulate their accomplishments and the emotions surrounding them. By documenting your journey, you not only create a tangible record of your progress but also cultivate a deeper understanding of your creative expression and artistry. Reflecting on your successes helps to combat self-doubt, providing clear evidence of your capabilities and the unique contributions you bring to the world. Over time, this habit can transform your perception of challenges, viewing them instead as opportunities for growth.

Engaging with your community is another powerful method for celebrating achievements. Sharing your successes with friends, family, or fellow creatives can enhance your sense of belonging and support. Life Path 3 individuals thrive in social environments, and surrounding yourself with people who appreciate your talents can amplify your joy. Organizing small gatherings, whether virtual or in-person, to showcase your work, share stories, or even host workshops can create a celebratory atmosphere that not only honors your achievements but also inspires others within your community.

In addition to personal reflection and community engagement, consider setting specific milestones to celebrate. This could involve breaking down larger goals into smaller, manageable tasks. As you accomplish each task, take the time to acknowledge your progress. This goal-setting technique aligns perfectly with the Life Path 3's dynamic nature, allowing for a continuous cycle of achievement and celebration. Whether it's completing a creative project, mastering a new skill, or enhancing your communication abilities, recognizing these milestones fosters a sense of accomplishment and reinforces your commitment to personal growth.

Lastly, integrating mindfulness practices into your celebration routine can enhance emotional well-being and positivity. Mindfulness encourages you to be present in the moment, allowing you to fully experience the joy of your achievements. Techniques such as meditation, deep breathing, or simply taking a moment to savor your success can deepen your appreciation for your journey. By practicing gratitude for your accomplishments, you not only honor your past efforts but also cultivate a positive outlook for future endeavors, creating a harmonious balance between your social life and personal growth.

Chapter 6

Balancing Social Life and Personal Growth

The Importance of Social Connections

Social connections play a pivotal role in the lives of individuals on Life Path 3, a path characterized by creativity, self-expression, and communication. These connections serve not only as a source of emotional support but also as platforms for personal growth and artistic development. For those who resonate with this life path, fostering relationships can enhance their creative output and provide opportunities for collaboration, idea exchange, and constructive feedback. Engaging with others can stimulate inspiration, allowing Life Path 3 individuals to tap into a deeper well of creativity that might remain dormant in isolation.

Building a network of supportive relationships can significantly impact the self-confidence of Life Path 3 individuals. As they navigate through challenges and self-doubt, having a circle of friends or mentors who encourage and validate their creative endeavors can fortify their belief in their abilities. This is especially important for Life Path 3 individuals, who may sometimes struggle with insecurity about their talents. The affirmation and encouragement from a community can act as a catalyst, propelling them to take risks, pursue new creative opportunities, and embrace their unique artistic voice.

Furthermore, the act of sharing one's creative journey with others fosters a sense of belonging and purpose. Life Path 3 individuals thrive in environments where they can express themselves freely and connect with like-minded people. This exchange of ideas not only enhances their own artistic expression but also contributes to a larger community dynamic. By participating in group projects or collaborative art initiatives, Life Path 3 individuals can experience the joy of collective creativity, which can be incredibly fulfilling and rewarding.

In addition to enhancing creativity, social connections offer Life Path 3 individuals the chance to develop essential communication skills. Engaging in conversations, attending workshops, or participating in community events can sharpen their ability to articulate thoughts and emotions effectively. These skills are crucial for Life Path 3 individuals, as their path encourages them to be expressive and articulate. By honing these abilities through interaction with others, they can convey their ideas more powerfully, thus amplifying their impact in both personal and professional spheres.

Ultimately, the importance of social connections extends beyond mere emotional support; it is about creating a holistic environment conducive to personal and artistic growth. Life Path 3 individuals are encouraged to prioritize nurturing relationships and building a supportive community. By doing so, they will not only unlock their true life potential but also cultivate joy, positivity, and a profound sense of fulfillment in their creative pursuits. Embracing the richness of social connections can transform their journey, leading to a more vibrant and meaningful life experience.

Setting Boundaries in Relationships

Setting boundaries in relationships is essential for individuals on Life Path 3, as it allows for the nurturing of creativity and personal growth. Boundaries serve as guidelines that help define what is acceptable behavior from others and protect one's emotional well-being. For creative individuals, having clear boundaries is particularly important because it fosters an environment where they can freely express their artistic impulses without fear of judgment or misunderstanding. Establishing these limits can encourage deeper, more authentic connections while simultaneously safeguarding the unique essence that Life Path 3 individuals bring to their relationships.

To effectively set boundaries, one must first engage in self-reflection. Understanding personal needs and desires is crucial for Life Path 3 individuals, who often prioritize social interactions and creative collaborations. Taking time to contemplate what feels comfortable and what does not can empower these individuals to articulate their boundaries clearly. This self-awareness not only enhances communication skills but also builds confidence, enabling them to voice their needs without guilt or hesitation.

Acknowledging one's own limits is the first step toward healthier interactions, allowing Life Path 3 individuals to create relationships that are mutually beneficial and supportive.

Communicating boundaries can be challenging, especially for those who are naturally inclined to please others. However, Life Path 3 individuals can benefit immensely from developing assertive communication techniques. This involves expressing one's thoughts and feelings openly while remaining respectful of others. Using "I" statements can be particularly effective, as they focus on personal experiences rather than placing blame. For instance, saying "I feel overwhelmed when I have too many commitments" is more constructive than saying "You always make me feel overwhelmed." This approach not only clarifies one's boundaries but also fosters a more constructive dialogue that can strengthen relationships.

It is important to recognize that setting boundaries may lead to discomfort, particularly in relationships where these limits have not been previously established. Life Path 3 individuals should be prepared for varied reactions from others, including resistance or misunderstanding. However, maintaining boundaries is a form of self-respect that ultimately contributes to healthier dynamics. By prioritizing their own well-being, Life Path 3 individuals can create space for joy, positivity, and deeper connections without compromising their creative spirit. Over time, those around them will learn to respect these boundaries, leading to more fulfilling interactions.

Finally, nurturing relationships while maintaining boundaries is a continuous process that requires ongoing effort and adjustment. Life Path 3 individuals should regularly evaluate their relationships and the boundaries they have set, ensuring they continue to align with their evolving needs and creative aspirations. This practice not only enhances emotional well-being but also promotes spiritual growth and a sense of purpose. By cultivating relationships that honor both individuality and connection, Life Path 3 individuals can thrive personally and artistically, ultimately unleashing their true life potential in all aspects of their lives.

Time Management for Personal Development

Time management is a crucial skill for individuals on Life Path 3, who often find themselves juggling creative projects, social engagements, and personal growth pursuits. Effective time management allows for the nurturing of artistic talents while simultaneously fostering personal development. By prioritizing tasks and setting clear goals, individuals can channel their creative energies into productive endeavors, enhancing both their artistry and emotional well-being. A structured approach to time management helps mitigate the chaos that can arise from an abundance of ideas and opportunities, allowing for a more focused and intentional life.

One effective technique for improving time management is the implementation of a daily or weekly planner. This tool can serve as a visual representation of one's commitments and aspirations. Life Path 3 individuals thrive on inspiration and spontaneity, but a planner can help balance these traits with the discipline needed for personal growth. By allocating specific time blocks for creative expression, social interactions, and self-care activities, individuals can ensure they are nurturing all aspects of their lives. Regularly reviewing and adjusting these plans fosters adaptability and encourages a proactive approach to time management.

Setting clear, achievable goals is another cornerstone of effective time management. For those on Life Path 3, these goals might encompass areas of creative expression, such as completing an art project or developing a new communication skill. Breaking down larger objectives into smaller, manageable tasks can alleviate the feelings of overwhelm that often accompany ambitious aspirations. By celebrating small victories along the way, individuals can build confidence and maintain motivation, reinforcing a positive mindset that is essential for personal development.

Moreover, cultivating a balance between social life and personal growth is particularly vital for Life Path 3 individuals, who often thrive in collaborative environments. While it is important to engage with others and share creative energies, time must also be set aside for introspection and self-improvement. Establishing boundaries around social commitments can create the necessary space for reflection and personal exploration. This balance enables individuals to cultivate meaningful relationships while ensuring that their personal development journey remains a priority.

Ultimately, mastering time management is not just about efficiency; it is about creating a life that aligns with one's values and aspirations. For Life Path 3 individuals, this means finding joy in the process of creation, building confidence through skill development, and fostering emotional well-being through mindfulness practices. By embracing time management as a tool for personal development, individuals can unlock their true potential, enhancing their creative expressions and nurturing the relationships that support their growth.

Chapter 7

Techniques for Enhancing Joy and Positivity

Gratitude Practices

Gratitude practices serve as a powerful tool for individuals on Life Path 3, enhancing their creative expression and overall emotional well-being. By cultivating gratitude, Life Path 3 individuals can effectively shift their focus from what may be lacking in their lives to appreciating the abundance that already exists. This shift not only fosters a more positive mindset but also enhances their ability to communicate and connect with others, a vital aspect of their life path. Regularly engaging in gratitude practices creates a fertile ground for creativity to flourish, allowing artistic ideas to emerge more effortlessly.

Implementing gratitude practices can be as simple as maintaining a daily gratitude journal. In this journal, Life Path 3 individuals can jot down three things they are grateful for each day, no matter how small. This exercise encourages mindfulness and reflection, enabling them to become more aware of the positive moments that often go unnoticed. Over time, this practice can help to overcome self-doubt by reinforcing the notion that there are always reasons to feel joyful and optimistic, even in challenging times. As they document their gratitude, they may find inspiration for new projects or ways to express themselves creatively.

Another effective gratitude practice involves expressing appreciation to others, which aligns perfectly with the social and communicative nature of Life Path 3. Writing thank-you notes or making a point to verbally acknowledge the contributions of friends, family, and colleagues can strengthen relationships and build community. These acts not only uplift the recipients but also enhance the giver's sense of connection and purpose. Such interactions can serve as a reminder that they are not alone on their journey, promoting a sense of belonging and support that is crucial for personal growth.

Mindfulness practices can also be integrated with gratitude exercises to deepen their impact. Simple techniques, such as guided meditations focused on gratitude, can help Life Path 3 individuals cultivate a more profound sense of appreciation for their experiences, relationships, and talents. These sessions can serve as a grounding practice, allowing them to explore their emotions and thoughts in a nurturing environment. By embracing gratitude within mindfulness, they can enhance their emotional well-being while also igniting their creative spirit, leading to more fulfilling artistic expressions.

Finally, setting goals that incorporate gratitude can enhance the pursuit of dreams and aspirations for Life Path 3 individuals. When they approach goal-setting with a mindset of gratitude, they are more likely to recognize the steps they have already taken toward achieving their dreams. This perspective not only boosts confidence but also encourages resilience in the face of challenges. By celebrating each small success along the way, they create a positive feedback loop that reinforces their belief in their abilities and the importance of their creative contributions to the world.

Cultivating a Positive Mindset

Cultivating a positive mindset is essential for individuals on Life Path 3, as it serves as a foundation for creativity and self-expression. A positive mindset not only enhances one's ability to communicate effectively but also fosters resilience against self-doubt. For numerologers, understanding the significance of mindset can help guide Life Path 3 individuals toward unlocking their true potential. By embracing positivity, they can navigate the challenges of personal growth and build stronger connections within their communities.

One of the key components of a positive mindset is the practice of gratitude. Individuals can start each day by acknowledging the things they are thankful for, no matter how small. This simple act shifts focus from negativity and fosters a worldview that appreciates abundance rather than scarcity. For those on Life Path 3, this practice can enhance creativity by encouraging a sense of wonder and inspiration that fuels artistic endeavors. Keeping a gratitude journal can also serve as a tangible reminder of the positive aspects of life, promoting an optimistic outlook.

Visualization techniques can further cultivate a positive mindset, especially for Life Path 3 individuals who thrive on creative expression. By picturing their goals and aspirations, they can create a mental image that motivates and energizes them. This practice not only enhances goal-setting efforts but also aligns with their artistic nature, allowing them to envision their future in vibrant detail. Engaging in visualization exercises regularly can help solidify a positive mindset, making the pursuit of dreams feel more attainable.

Additionally, surrounding oneself with encouraging and supportive individuals is crucial in nurturing positivity. Life Path 3 individuals often shine brightest when they are part of a vibrant community that uplifts and inspires them. By building relationships with like-minded people, they can foster an environment conducive to personal and artistic growth. These connections can serve as a source of motivation, helping to combat the feelings of self-doubt that may arise. Collaborating with others can also spark new ideas and enhance creative expression, further reinforcing a positive mindset.

Incorporating mindfulness practices into daily routines can significantly contribute to cultivating a positive mindset. Techniques such as meditation, deep breathing, or mindful walks can help reduce stress and enhance emotional well-being. For Life Path 3 individuals, these practices provide a space for reflection and self-discovery, allowing them to connect with their inner selves. By grounding themselves in the present moment, they can shift their focus away from negative thoughts and cultivate a more balanced perspective, ultimately supporting their journey toward achieving their dreams and fulfilling their life purpose.

Engaging in Joyful Activities

Engaging in joyful activities is essential for individuals on Life Path 3, as it fosters creativity and self-expression. Joy is a powerful catalyst that not only enhances emotional well-being but also serves as a conduit for artistic inspiration. People with this life path often thrive in environments that celebrate spontaneity and playfulness. Incorporating joyful activities into daily routines can significantly elevate the quality of life and enable those on this path to embrace their innate creativity. From painting to dancing or even engaging in playful conversations, each joyful interaction contributes to a vibrant expression of their unique essence.

One effective way to engage in joyful activities is through the exploration of various artistic mediums. Life Path 3 individuals are often drawn to creative outlets such as painting, writing, acting, or music. Dedicating time to explore these artistic endeavors can lead to profound personal discoveries. For instance, participating in a community art class not only enhances skills but also fosters connections with like-minded individuals. This communal aspect is crucial, as it allows Life Path 3 individuals to share their joy and creativity, thereby nurturing their relationships and building a supportive community.

In addition to artistic expression, incorporating physical activities that bring joy can be transformative. Activities like dancing, yoga, or hiking allow for self-expression while also promoting physical health. These activities encourage participants to connect with their bodies, releasing pent-up emotions and inviting joy into the present moment. The exhilaration derived from movement can stimulate creativity, prompting new ideas and inspirations that can be channeled into artistic pursuits. Thus, balancing physical engagement with creative expression leads to a holistic approach to personal growth.

Mindfulness practices play an integral role in enhancing joy and positivity in daily life. Life Path 3 individuals can benefit from techniques such as meditation, deep breathing exercises, or gratitude journaling. These practices cultivate a deeper awareness of the present moment, allowing for a more profound appreciation of life's simple pleasures. By consciously acknowledging joyful experiences, individuals can shift their focus away from self-doubt and negativity, creating a fertile ground for confidence and creativity to flourish. This mindful approach reinforces the understanding that joy is not merely a fleeting emotion but a sustained state of being that invites more positivity into one's life.

Finally, setting goals around joyful activities can be a powerful motivator for Life Path 3 individuals. By establishing specific, achievable objectives related to creative pursuits or social engagements, individuals can track their progress and celebrate their achievements. This process not only enhances feelings of accomplishment but also reinforces the importance of joy in their lives. As they continue to pursue their passions and engage in uplifting activities, they will find themselves more aligned with their true potential, ultimately leading to a fulfilling and vibrant life.

Chapter 8

Career Paths and Opportunities

Identifying Career Options for Life Path 3

Identifying career options for individuals on Life Path 3 involves recognizing their inherent creative talents and communicative abilities. Life Path 3 is characterized by a vibrant expression of creativity, making careers that allow for artistic expression particularly suitable. Professions in the arts, such as acting, writing, or visual arts, can provide a fulfilling outlet for their imaginative energies. These careers not only allow for self-expression but also enable Life Path 3 individuals to connect with others through their work, fostering a sense of community and shared experience.

In addition to artistic pursuits, Life Path 3 individuals may find fulfillment in careers that emphasize communication and interpersonal skills. Fields such as public relations, marketing, teaching, or counseling can be ideal, as they allow for the use of their natural charisma and ability to engage others. These careers often involve storytelling and the sharing of ideas, which resonate deeply with the Life Path 3's love for language and connection. Exploring options within these domains can lead to rewarding pathways that align with their strengths.

Entrepreneurship can also be a viable route for Life Path 3 individuals, as it provides the flexibility to create and innovate according to their vision. Many successful entrepreneurs have a Life Path 3 designation, leveraging their creativity to develop unique products or services. This path allows them to embrace their individuality while also building a brand that reflects their personal values and artistic inclinations. By combining their creative spirit with business acumen, they can carve out a niche that showcases their talents.

While exploring career options, it is crucial for Life Path 3 individuals to consider roles that encourage collaboration and community-building. Careers in event planning, social work, or community organization can satisfy their desire for social interaction and support. These roles not only allow them to work creatively but also enable them to uplift and inspire others, fulfilling their innate need to contribute positively to the lives of those around them. Such environments can help mitigate self-doubt and bolster their confidence as they see the impact of their work.

Ultimately, identifying the right career path for Life Path 3 requires a balance between creative expression and practical application. By aligning their career choices with their passions and strengths, they can cultivate a sense of joy and fulfillment in their work. Whether pursuing traditional artistic careers, engaging in communication-focused roles, or exploring entrepreneurial ventures, Life

Path 3 individuals have a wealth of opportunities to tap into. Embracing this journey with an open heart and mind will enable them to unleash their true potential and contribute meaningfully to the world.

Leveraging Creativity in the Workplace

Creativity is an essential component of a thriving workplace, particularly for individuals on the Life Path 3 journey, who are naturally inclined toward artistic expression and innovative thinking. Leveraging creativity within the workplace can transform not only personal experiences but also the overall environment, fostering collaboration and enhancing productivity. Life Path 3 individuals can harness their innate talents to inspire others, develop unique solutions to challenges, and cultivate a vibrant atmosphere where creativity flourishes. By embracing creative practices, they can also help establish a culture that values and rewards innovative thinking.

One effective way to leverage creativity in the workplace is through open communication and brainstorming sessions. Encouraging team members to share their ideas without fear of judgment allows for a free flow of thoughts and fosters an inclusive environment. Life Path 3 individuals, known for their exceptional communication skills, can take the lead in facilitating these discussions, ensuring that everyone feels heard and valued. This collaborative approach not only stimulates creativity but also strengthens relationships among coworkers, ultimately leading to a more cohesive team dynamic.

In addition to open communication, incorporating creative problem-solving techniques can enhance the workplace experience. Life Path 3 individuals can utilize their imaginative nature to approach challenges from different angles, encouraging their peers to think outside the box. Techniques such as mind mapping, role-playing scenarios, and visual brainstorming can help unlock new perspectives and solutions. By introducing these methods, they can empower others to tap into their creativity, resulting in innovative outcomes that benefit the entire organization.

Moreover, creating a stimulating physical environment can significantly impact creativity in the workplace. Life Path 3 individuals can advocate for spaces that inspire and motivate. This might include incorporating art, greenery, or even flexible workspaces that allow for movement and collaboration. A well-designed environment can ignite inspiration and encourage spontaneous interactions among team members, leading to breakthroughs in creativity and productivity. By prioritizing such an atmosphere, individuals on this life path can help cultivate a workplace where creativity is not only welcomed but celebrated.

Finally, mindfulness practices play a crucial role in enhancing creativity and emotional well-being in the workplace. Life Path 3 individuals can introduce techniques such as meditation, breathing exercises, or moments of reflection to help colleagues manage stress and unlock their creative potential. By emphasizing the importance of mental clarity and emotional balance, they can foster a culture that values well-being alongside productivity. This holistic approach not only nurtures individual creativity but also strengthens the collective spirit of the workplace, leading to a more fulfilling and successful environment for everyone involved.

Building a Fulfilling Career

Building a fulfilling career is a crucial aspect for individuals on Life Path 3, where creativity and self-expression play a significant role. As a Life Path 3 individual, you possess a unique blend of artistic talent, communication skills, and charisma that can be harnessed to create a professional life that resonates with your inner passions. It is important to identify career paths that not only align with your creative abilities but also allow you to express your authentic self. Exploring various fields such as art, writing, performance, or even entrepreneurship can lead to a career that is both satisfying and fulfilling.

To embark on this journey, start by assessing your strengths and interests. Engage in self-reflection to clarify what drives you and what forms of creative expression speak to your spirit. Consider taking personality assessments or career aptitude tests that focus on creativity and communication, as these can provide insights into potential career paths. Additionally, seek inspiration from successful individuals in fields that excite you. Their stories can offer valuable lessons and motivate you to pursue your own unique path in a career that feels meaningful.

As you navigate your career, developing robust communication skills is essential for effective collaboration and networking. Life Path 3 individuals often thrive in environments where they can share ideas and connect with others. Attend workshops or seminars focused on enhancing communication skills. Practicing public speaking, active listening, and persuasive writing can significantly improve your ability to convey your ideas and engage with diverse audiences. Building these skills will not only enhance your professional opportunities but also help you foster deeper connections in your personal life.

Overcoming self-doubt is another challenge that many on Life Path 3 face, especially when pursuing creative endeavors. Cultivating confidence is vital to achieving your career aspirations. Engage in techniques that promote positive self-talk and visualizations of success. Surround yourself with supportive individuals who encourage your creative pursuits and provide constructive feedback. By embracing a mindset of growth and resilience, you can transform self-doubt into a catalyst for personal and professional development.

Lastly, balancing your social life with personal growth is key to maintaining overall well-being while building a fulfilling career. Life Path 3 individuals often thrive in social settings, yet it is crucial to carve out time for introspection and skill development. Set clear goals for your career and personal life, and prioritize activities that align with these objectives. Mindfulness practices can be integrated into your daily routine, helping you stay grounded and focused. By nurturing your relationships while pursuing your creative passions, you can cultivate a fulfilling career that brings joy, purpose, and a sense of community.

Chapter 9

Nurturing Relationships and Building Community

The Role of Relationships in Personal Growth

The intricate tapestry of relationships plays a pivotal role in personal growth, particularly for individuals on Life Path 3. Relationships serve as mirrors, reflecting not only our strengths and talents but also areas where we can develop and evolve. For those who resonate with the creative spirit of Life Path 3, these connections can provide invaluable feedback and encouragement, fostering an environment where artistic expression flourishes. Engaging with others allows for the exchange of ideas, which can spark new insights and inspire creativity, pushing individuals to explore their full potential.

As Life Path 3 individuals are often natural communicators, nurturing relationships can significantly enhance their ability to articulate thoughts and emotions. Building strong connections with others cultivates a supportive atmosphere where individuals can practice and refine their communication skills. Through dialogue and interaction, they learn to express themselves more clearly, overcome limitations, and convey their unique perspectives. This development is crucial, as effective communication not only enhances personal relationships but also opens doors in professional contexts, allowing for greater collaboration and opportunities in creative fields.

Overcoming self-doubt is another critical aspect of personal growth for those on Life Path 3, and relationships play a crucial role in this journey. Supportive friends and mentors can provide encouragement and validation, helping individuals recognize their worth and capabilities. When surrounded by positive influences, Life Path 3 individuals are more likely to take risks in their creative endeavors, experiment with new ideas, and embrace their authenticity. These relationships serve as a foundation for building confidence, empowering them to pursue their passions without the weight of fear holding them back.

Balancing social life with personal growth is essential for maintaining emotional well-being. Individuals on Life Path 3 often thrive in social settings, finding joy in connecting with others. However, it is equally important to carve out time for introspection and self-discovery. Cultivating a network that understands this balance can help Life Path 3 individuals prioritize their personal growth while still enjoying the richness of their social lives. By engaging in meaningful conversations and shared experiences, they can foster relationships that encourage both companionship and self-exploration.

In addition to nurturing personal development, relationships can significantly contribute to the broader community. For Life Path 3 individuals, the act of building connections with others can lead to collaborative artistic ventures, community projects, and opportunities for service. Engaging with like-minded individuals not only enhances their creative output but also reinforces a sense of belonging and purpose. Ultimately, embracing the role of relationships in personal growth allows those on Life Path 3 to unleash their creative spirit, harnessing the power of connection to achieve their dreams and aspirations.

Creating a Supportive Network

Building a supportive network is a fundamental aspect of nurturing your creative spirit as a Life Path 3 individual. This journey is not meant to be walked alone; rather, it thrives in the company of like-minded souls who share your aspirations and passions. Surrounding yourself with a diverse group of people, including fellow artists, mentors, and supportive friends, can significantly enhance your creative expression and provide you with the encouragement needed to pursue your goals. Each connection offers a unique perspective that can help you unlock your true life potential, making it essential to intentionally cultivate these relationships.

In the world of creative expression and artistry, collaboration can lead to remarkable breakthroughs. Engaging with other creatives allows for the exchange of ideas and techniques, fostering an atmosphere where innovation can flourish. Whether it's through attending workshops, participating in group projects, or joining local art collectives, immersing yourself in a community of artists can inspire you to explore new avenues of creativity. This interconnectedness not only enhances your artistic skills but also strengthens your confidence, as you realize that you are part of a larger tapestry of creativity.

Effective communication is another critical aspect of creating a supportive network. As a Life Path 3, you possess natural charisma and expressiveness, traits that can facilitate meaningful connections. However, it is essential to hone your communication skills to articulate your thoughts and feelings clearly. Actively listening to others, providing constructive feedback, and sharing your own experiences can deepen your relationships and foster an environment of mutual respect and understanding. When you communicate openly, you encourage others to do the same, creating a safe space for vulnerability and growth.

Overcoming self-doubt is often a shared struggle among creatives, and a supportive network can be instrumental in this regard. When you connect with others who have faced similar challenges, you can share strategies for building confidence and overcoming obstacles. Celebrating each other's achievements, no matter how small, reinforces a positive mindset and cultivates joy within your community. By being part of a network that uplifts and encourages, you not only enhance your emotional well-being but also contribute to the collective growth of the group.

Finally, nurturing relationships within your supportive network requires effort and intention. Regular check-ins, shared experiences, and collaborative projects strengthen these bonds and create a sense of belonging. Balancing your social life and personal growth is essential, as meaningful connections can significantly enhance your overall well-being. As you invest in these relationships, you will find that they not only support your artistic endeavors but also enrich your journey toward spiritual growth and finding purpose. A vibrant, supportive network ultimately serves as a foundation for achieving your dreams and living a fulfilling life as a Life Path 3.

Engaging with Your Community

Engaging with your community is an essential aspect of realizing the full potential of Life Path 3. This life path is characterized by creativity, communication, and social interaction, making community engagement a natural extension of your personal growth and artistic expression. By actively participating in your community, you not only enhance your own life but also contribute to the collective well-being and creativity of those around you. This symbiotic relationship can lead to new opportunities and inspire further artistic endeavors, ultimately enriching your journey as a Life Path 3 individual.

To effectively engage with your community, it is crucial to identify spaces that resonate with your interests and values. Attend local art shows, workshops, or community events that align with your creative pursuits. Collaborating with fellow artists or engaging in group projects can foster a sense of belonging and provide a platform for your ideas. This exposure not only nurtures your creative spirit but also helps you develop essential communication skills, allowing you to articulate your vision and connect with others on a deeper level.

Moreover, overcoming self-doubt is a common challenge for those on Life Path 3, and community engagement can play a pivotal role in building confidence. By sharing your work and ideas with others, you receive valuable feedback that can affirm your talents and encourage you to take risks in your artistry. The support and encouragement from a community can help dismantle the barriers of self-doubt, allowing you to express yourself more freely and authentically. This interaction fosters a positive atmosphere where creativity flourishes, leading to personal and artistic growth.

Balancing social life with personal growth can be particularly rewarding when you actively engage with your community. Seek out opportunities that allow you to connect with like-minded individuals who share your passions. This not only enhances your social life but also encourages you to develop new skills and perspectives that contribute to your overall well-being. As you cultivate these relationships, you will find that they provide both inspiration and motivation, enabling you to pursue your dreams with renewed vigor and optimism.

Finally, mindfulness practices can greatly enhance your emotional well-being while engaging with your community. Being present in social interactions allows you to appreciate the connections you are building and the experiences you are sharing. Incorporating mindfulness into your community involvement helps you remain grounded and open to new ideas, fostering a joyful and positive atmosphere. By nurturing these relationships and actively participating in your community, you create a supportive network that not only uplifts you but also magnifies the beauty of your creative expression, leading to a more fulfilling life on your journey as a Life Path 3.

Chapter 10

Mindfulness Practices for Emotional Well-Being

Introduction to Mindfulness

Mindfulness, a practice rooted in ancient traditions, has gained significant attention in contemporary society for its profound impact on emotional well-being and personal growth. For individuals on Life Path 3, which emphasizes creativity, self-expression, and social engagement, mindfulness serves as a powerful tool to enhance these core attributes. By cultivating present-moment awareness, Life Path 3 individuals can tap into their innate creativity and articulate their thoughts and feelings more effectively. This subchapter aims to explore how mindfulness can unlock the true potential of those on this path, fostering both personal and interpersonal growth.

At its essence, mindfulness involves paying deliberate attention to thoughts, emotions, and sensations without judgment. This practice encourages individuals to observe their internal experiences and the world around them, promoting a deeper understanding of oneself and the environment. For Life Path 3 individuals, who often grapple with self-doubt and the pressures of creative expression, mindfulness can act as a stabilizing force. By learning to observe rather than react, they can navigate their emotions and thoughts with greater clarity, leading to increased confidence in their creative endeavors and communication skills.

Integrating mindfulness into daily life can significantly enhance the creative process. Engaging in activities such as mindful breathing, meditation, or even mindful walking allows Life Path 3 individuals to clear mental clutter and access their creative reservoir. This heightened state of awareness can spark inspiration and innovative ideas, making it easier to express oneself artistically. Additionally, mindfulness fosters a sense of joy and positivity, essential qualities for those who thrive on social interaction and community building. By being fully present, individuals can cultivate more meaningful relationships, enriching their social life while simultaneously nurturing their own personal growth.

The practice of mindfulness also plays a pivotal role in overcoming challenges associated with self-doubt. By developing a non-judgmental awareness of one's thoughts and feelings, individuals on Life Path 3 can learn to challenge negative self-talk and build resilience. This process promotes emotional well-being, allowing for a more balanced approach to life's ups and downs. As they become more adept at recognizing and managing their emotions, they are better equipped to set and achieve personal and professional goals, opening doors to fulfilling career opportunities that align with their creative spirit.

In summary, mindfulness is an invaluable practice that aligns seamlessly with the journey of Life Path 3 individuals. It enhances creative expression, fosters emotional well-being, and supports personal development. By incorporating mindfulness techniques into their lives, individuals can cultivate a deeper connection with themselves and their surroundings, ultimately leading to a more joyful, confident, and purpose-driven existence. Embracing mindfulness not only amplifies the creative journey but also enriches relationships and nurtures community, making it a cornerstone for anyone seeking to unleash their creative spirit.

Mindfulness Techniques for Daily Life

Mindfulness techniques can be a transformative tool for individuals on Life Path 3, as they enhance creative expression, boost communication skills, and foster a deeper connection with oneself and others. Incorporating mindfulness into daily life encourages a heightened awareness of thoughts, emotions, and surroundings, which is essential for those who seek to unlock their true potential. By practicing mindfulness, Life Path 3 individuals can cultivate a positive mindset that nurtures their creative spirit and supports their journey toward personal growth and self-actualization.

One effective mindfulness technique is the practice of mindful breathing. This simple yet powerful exercise involves focusing on the breath as it flows in and out of the body. Life Path 3 individuals can set aside a few moments each day to engage in this practice, allowing themselves to detach from distractions and center their thoughts. By concentrating on the rhythm of their breath, they can create a calming environment that fosters creativity and clarity. This technique not only reduces stress but also enhances emotional well-being, making it easier to overcome self-doubt and build confidence in their artistic abilities.

Another valuable mindfulness practice is the technique of mindful observation. This involves taking the time to notice the details of one's surroundings without judgment. Life Path 3 individuals can benefit from spending time in nature or engaging with their immediate environment, allowing themselves to fully experience the sights, sounds, and textures around them. This practice not only stimulates creativity but also enhances communication skills, as it encourages a deeper understanding of the world and the people within it. By observing without the interference of preconceived notions, individuals can foster empathy and connection in their relationships.

Incorporating gratitude into daily mindfulness practices can also significantly enhance positivity and joy. Life Path 3 individuals can create a gratitude journal where they note things they are thankful for each day. This simple act of reflection helps shift focus away from negativity and cultivates a mindset of abundance. By regularly acknowledging the positive aspects of their lives, they can inspire themselves and others, thereby nurturing relationships and building a supportive community.

Gratitude fosters a sense of fulfillment that is vital for personal growth and spiritual development.

Finally, practicing mindfulness through creative expression can be particularly beneficial for those on Life Path 3. Engaging in artistic activities such as painting, writing, or dancing with full awareness allows individuals to tap into their creative spirit while remaining present in the moment. This not only encourages the exploration of new ideas but also reinforces the joy of creation, which is central to the Life Path 3 experience. By integrating these mindfulness techniques into their daily lives, individuals can enhance their emotional well-being, achieve their dreams, and find a deeper sense of purpose in their creative journeys.

Benefits of Mindfulness for Life Path 3

Mindfulness offers a plethora of benefits tailored specifically to individuals on Life Path 3, who are often characterized by their creativity, sociability, and expressive nature. By embracing mindfulness practices, those on this path can enhance their creative expression, allowing their artistic talents to flourish. Mindfulness encourages individuals to be fully present in the moment, which can lead to a deeper connection with their creative impulses. This heightened awareness not only fosters inspiration but also enables Life Path 3 individuals to channel their emotions into their artistic work, ultimately leading to more authentic and engaging creations.

In addition to enhancing creativity, mindfulness assists Life Path 3 individuals in developing their communication skills.

Effective communication is a hallmark of this life path, and mindfulness can help refine the ability to listen actively and respond thoughtfully. By practicing mindfulness, individuals can cultivate a deeper understanding of their own thoughts and feelings, allowing them to articulate their ideas more clearly. This clarity in communication not only strengthens personal and professional relationships but also aids in overcoming self-doubt, as individuals become more attuned to their inner dialogue and learn to express themselves with confidence.

Another significant benefit of mindfulness for Life Path 3 is its role in balancing social life and personal growth. Those on this path often thrive in social settings, yet they may struggle with the pressure to maintain a vibrant social life while pursuing personal development. Mindfulness encourages individuals to reflect on their social interactions and assess their emotional needs. By embracing mindfulness, Life Path 3 individuals can prioritize meaningful connections and create a supportive community while also dedicating time to their personal growth and self-care.

Mindfulness practices can also enhance joy and positivity, which are essential for individuals on Life Path 3. By being present and appreciating the moment, individuals can cultivate an optimistic outlook on life. Mindful practices such as gratitude journaling and meditation can help shift focus from negative thoughts to positive experiences. This shift in perspective not only elevates emotional well-being but also encourages a more profound appreciation for life's simple pleasures, contributing significantly to overall happiness and fulfillment.

Finally, incorporating mindfulness into daily routines can serve as a powerful tool for goal setting and achieving dreams for Life Path 3 individuals. Mindfulness fosters a greater awareness of one's aspirations and motivations, enabling individuals to set intentions that align with their true selves. By remaining present and mindful, they can navigate challenges with resilience and clarity, ensuring that their creative pursuits and career paths resonate with their authentic desires. This intentional approach not only propels them toward their goals but also enriches their journey with purpose and meaning.

Chapter 11: Goal Setting and Achieving Dreams

The Importance of Goals

Goals play a crucial role in the journey of individuals on Life Path 3, as they serve as a roadmap guiding creative expression and personal development. For those who resonate with this path, setting clear and achievable goals can enhance the natural talents and skills that define their artistic and communicative abilities. By establishing specific targets, individuals can channel their creativity into structured endeavors, ensuring that their expressive potential does not remain dormant. These goals not only provide direction but also foster a sense of purpose, which is essential for maintaining motivation and focus throughout the creative process.

The act of goal setting enables Life Path 3 individuals to overcome self-doubt and build confidence in their abilities. When aspirations are articulated and broken down into manageable steps, the overwhelming nature of creative pursuits diminishes. Achieving smaller, incremental goals can create a positive feedback loop, reinforcing self-belief and encouraging further exploration of one's creative identity. This process is vital for maintaining enthusiasm and a sense of achievement, as it transforms abstract desires into tangible accomplishments, anchoring the individual in their creative journey.

Balance is a key theme for those on Life Path 3, where social interactions and personal growth must coexist harmoniously. By setting goals that encompass both creative endeavors and personal development, individuals can cultivate a well-rounded existence. For instance, goals might include dedicating time to artistic projects while also seeking opportunities for social connection and community building. This balanced approach not only enhances the quality of social relationships but also nurtures the individual's emotional well-being, creating a supportive environment where both creativity and personal growth can flourish.

Additionally, the pursuit of goals aligns closely with enhancing joy and positivity in the lives of Life Path 3 individuals. Goals infused with personal significance can act as catalysts for joy, as they inspire individuals to engage deeply with their passions. This engagement fosters a positive mindset, as the act of pursuing dreams and aspirations generates vitality and enthusiasm. Moreover, by setting goals focused on mindfulness and emotional well-being, individuals can learn to navigate the complexities of their emotional landscape, ensuring that their creative expression is not only fulfilling but also sustainable.

Lastly, the integration of goal setting into the creative process opens up a myriad of career paths and opportunities for Life Path 3 individuals. By identifying professional aspirations that align with their unique talents and values, individuals can create a fulfilling career that resonates with their innate creativity. This proactive approach to career development empowers them to seek out opportunities that not only utilize their skills but also contribute to their personal growth and community engagement. Ultimately, the importance of goals cannot be overstated; they serve as foundational pillars that support the artistic, emotional, and spiritual aspirations of those walking the Life Path 3 journey.

SMART Goal Setting

SMART goal setting is a transformative approach that aligns perfectly with the creative essence of Life Path 3 individuals. SMART, an acronym for Specific, Measurable, Achievable, Relevant, and Time-bound, provides a structured framework that can help Life Path 3s channel their creative energies into actionable outcomes. For those on this path, who often thrive in expressing themselves artistically and socially, setting SMART goals can provide clarity and direction, ensuring that their creative endeavors do not become scattered or overwhelming.

Specificity is the first pillar of SMART goals. For Life Path 3 individuals, this means defining exactly what you want to achieve in your creative pursuits. Instead of setting a vague goal like "I want to be a better artist," a specific goal would be "I want to complete a series of five paintings that explore themes of joy and community." This clear focus allows Life Path 3s to tap into their natural creativity while ensuring that their efforts are directed toward a tangible outcome, enhancing their ability to express their artistic visions effectively.

Next is measurability. Life Path 3s can benefit from quantifying their goals to track progress and celebrate achievements. Instead of simply stating a desire to improve communication skills, a measurable goal could be "I will join a public speaking group and deliver at least three presentations over the next six months." This approach not only provides a clear metric for success but also fosters the confidence that Life Path 3s often need to overcome self-doubt. Celebrating these measurable milestones can reinforce positive feelings and encourage further creative expression.

Achievability is crucial when setting goals, especially for Life Path 3s who may sometimes set aspirations that feel overwhelming. It's essential to ensure that goals are realistic and attainable, considering current skills and resources. For example, a Life Path 3 might aim to participate in a local art exhibition rather than striving for a solo show in a prestigious gallery right away. This helps build confidence incrementally and allows for personal growth, creating a sustainable path toward larger ambitions while nurturing creative expression.

Lastly, setting time-bound goals is vital for maintaining motivation and focus. Life Path 3 individuals often thrive in dynamic environments, and having deadlines can help to channel their creative energy effectively. For instance, setting a timeline to complete a collaborative project with peers can foster a sense of community while ensuring that creativity is consistently engaged. By incorporating these elements of SMART goal setting, Life Path 3s can not only achieve their dreams but also cultivate joy and positivity in their journey, ultimately aligning their creative pursuits with their deeper life purpose.

Tracking Progress and Staying Motivated

Tracking progress is essential for anyone on the journey of self-discovery, especially for those embodying the creative spirit of Life Path 3. This path is characterized by expression, joy, and communication, making it crucial to establish tangible methods for monitoring growth. Keeping a journal can serve as an excellent tool for documenting daily experiences, creative endeavors, and emotional fluctuations. By reflecting on entries over time, individuals can identify patterns in their artistic expression and communication skills, allowing them to recognize areas of strength and opportunities for improvement.

In addition to journaling, setting specific, measurable goals can help Life Path 3 individuals maintain focus and motivation. These goals can range from completing a creative project to enhancing interpersonal skills or even building a more robust social network. Breaking larger objectives into smaller, manageable tasks makes it easier to track progress and celebrate small victories along the way. Celebrating these milestones reinforces positive behavior and encourages continued effort, creating a feedback loop that fosters motivation and creativity.

Staying motivated can be particularly challenging when self-doubt creeps in. Developing a practice of self-affirmation can counteract negative thoughts and bolster confidence. Life Path 3 individuals thrive on encouragement, so surrounding themselves with supportive friends and mentors can amplify their creative energy. Joining community groups, attending workshops, or participating in artistic collaborations can enhance motivation by providing external validation and inspiration. These connections not only nurture creativity but also contribute to a sense of belonging, which is vital for personal growth.

Mindfulness practices can also play a significant role in maintaining motivation and emotional well-being. Techniques such as meditation, deep breathing, and visualization can help individuals center themselves, reduce anxiety, and stay present in their creative pursuits. By cultivating awareness of their thoughts and emotions, Life Path 3 individuals can better understand their motivations and fears, allowing them to navigate challenges with resilience. This emotional clarity fosters a more profound connection to their creative spirit, enabling them to pursue their passions with renewed vigor.

Ultimately, the journey of tracking progress and staying motivated is a dynamic process filled with opportunities for growth and self-discovery. For Life Path 3 individuals, embracing creativity, communication, and community can lead to fulfilling experiences that enhance their personal and artistic lives. By establishing effective tracking methods, setting clear goals, nurturing supportive relationships, and practicing mindfulness, they can unlock their true potential and embark on a fulfilling path of continuous improvement and self-expression.

Chapter 12: Spiritual Growth and Finding Purpose

Exploring Spirituality

Exploring spirituality is a vital aspect of the journey for individuals on Life Path 3, as it intertwines with creativity and self-expression. Spirituality offers a pathway to connect with the deeper aspects of oneself, promoting a sense of purpose and direction. Engaging with spiritual practices can inspire creative ideas and foster an environment where artistic expression flourishes. By exploring spirituality, Life Path 3 individuals can tap into their innate gifts, allowing their creativity to be an extension of their spiritual journey.

Incorporating mindfulness practices into daily routines can significantly enhance emotional well-being for those on Life Path 3. Mindfulness encourages individuals to be present in the moment, cultivating a deeper awareness of their thoughts and feelings. This heightened awareness can lead to a more profound understanding of personal motivations and desires, enabling Life Path 3 individuals to align their creative pursuits with their spiritual goals. Simple mindfulness techniques, such as meditation or breathwork, can serve as powerful tools for grounding oneself and reducing anxiety, ultimately nurturing a more positive outlook on life.

The exploration of spirituality also involves delving into the concept of community and relationships. For individuals on Life Path 3, fostering connections with like-minded individuals can create a supportive environment that nurtures both creativity and spiritual growth. Building community not only enriches personal experiences but also enhances collaborative opportunities in artistic endeavors. Engaging in group activities, workshops, or spiritual gatherings can allow Life Path 3 individuals to share their insights and learn from others, further deepening their understanding of their spiritual paths.

Overcoming self-doubt is another crucial component within the spiritual exploration for Life Path 3. Spiritual practices can provide a solid foundation for building self-confidence and self-acceptance. By recognizing the inherent value of their creative expressions, individuals can embrace their unique perspectives and contributions to the world. This journey involves reframing negative thoughts and employing affirmations that resonate with their spiritual beliefs, thereby fostering a more empowered mindset essential for achieving their dreams and aspirations.

Ultimately, the exploration of spirituality serves as a transformative experience for Life Path 3 individuals, guiding them toward greater self-discovery and fulfillment.

By integrating spiritual practices into their lives, they can enhance their creative expression, develop robust communication skills, and create a balanced approach to social interactions and personal growth. Embracing this spiritual journey not only enriches their artistry but also illuminates their path to achieving their true potential, allowing them to thrive in all aspects of life.

Connecting with Your Higher Self

Connecting with your higher self is a transformative process that can significantly enhance the creative expression and overall life experience of individuals on a Life Path 3. This journey begins with the understanding that your higher self embodies your true essence, creativity, and wisdom. As a Life Path 3, your inherent gifts of communication and artistry can be channeled more effectively when you align with this deeper aspect of yourself. Engaging in consistent self-reflection and mindfulness practices can facilitate this connection, allowing you to access inspiration and clarity that fuels your creative endeavors.

To connect with your higher self, it is essential to cultivate an environment that encourages introspection and openness. Create a dedicated space for meditation or quiet time, free from distractions. In this space, practice techniques such as deep breathing, visualization, or journaling to deepen your self-awareness. These practices not only help silence the noise of everyday life but also create a pathway for intuition and creativity to emerge. As you explore your thoughts and feelings, you may discover profound insights that resonate with your artistic pursuits and personal growth.

In addition to personal reflection, engaging with nature can significantly enhance your connection to your higher self. Nature has a unique way of grounding us and inspiring creativity. Spend time outdoors, whether through walks, hikes, or simply sitting in a park, and observe the beauty around you. Allow the tranquility of the natural world to inspire your thoughts and creative expressions. This immersion in nature can also serve as a reminder of your interconnectedness with the universe, reinforcing your sense of purpose and joy.

Building relationships with like-minded individuals can further support your journey toward connecting with your higher self. Seek out communities that align with your interests in creativity, spirituality, and personal development. Sharing your experiences and insights with others can provide encouragement and help you overcome self-doubt. As you nurture these connections, you will find that collaboration and communication with others can amplify your creative spirit, allowing you to explore new ideas and perspectives that enrich your artistry.

Ultimately, connecting with your higher self is a continuous journey that requires commitment and practice. Embrace the process of self-discovery and the exploration of your inner world. As you deepen this connection, you will uncover a wellspring of creativity, confidence, and purpose that can profoundly influence not only your artistic endeavors but also your overall life experience as a Life Path

3. By fostering this relationship, you will be better equipped to navigate challenges, set meaningful goals, and achieve the dreams that resonate with your true self.

Living a Purpose-Driven Life

Living a purpose-driven life is a cornerstone for individuals on Life Path 3, who are often characterized by their creativity, expressive nature, and social charisma. This subchapter delves into the significance of aligning personal values and passions with daily actions to cultivate a fulfilling existence. For Life Path 3 individuals, this alignment often manifests through artistic endeavors and meaningful communication, serving as a conduit for self-expression and connection with others. By identifying what truly resonates with their inner selves, they can channel their creativity in ways that not only bring joy but also contribute positively to their communities.

A key aspect of living purposefully involves the continuous exploration of one's passions and talents. Life Path 3 individuals are naturally drawn to artistic pursuits, whether through visual arts, writing, or performance. Engaging in creative activities not only enhances their self-expression but also fosters a deeper understanding of their purpose. By dedicating time to explore various forms of creativity, they can discover which mediums resonate most with their authentic self, providing clarity and direction in their life journey. This exploration is essential, as it helps to eliminate self-doubt and builds confidence in their unique abilities.

Building a supportive community is another vital component of a purpose-driven life for those on Life Path 3. This life path is inherently social, and establishing nurturing relationships can amplify their creative energies. By surrounding themselves with like-minded individuals who share similar values and aspirations, Life Path 3 individuals can create a network that encourages collaboration and inspiration. These connections not only enhance personal growth but also create opportunities for collective artistic expression, fostering an environment where creativity can thrive.

Mindfulness practices play a crucial role in maintaining emotional well-being and enhancing joy for Life Path 3 individuals. Incorporating techniques such as meditation, journaling, or engaging in nature can help center their thoughts and emotions, allowing for greater clarity regarding their life purpose. By grounding themselves in the present moment, they can cultivate a positive mindset that nurtures creativity and inspires action toward their goals. These practices also assist in balancing their social lives with personal growth, ensuring they remain aligned with their true selves amidst external distractions.

Finally, effective goal setting is essential for Life Path 3 individuals seeking to achieve their dreams while living a purpose-driven life. By establishing clear, actionable goals that reflect their passions, they can create a roadmap that guides their journey. This process involves not only defining what success looks like but also breaking down larger aspirations into manageable steps. Regularly revisiting these goals and celebrating small achievements fosters a sense of progress and motivates continued effort. Through this focused approach, Life Path 3 individuals can navigate their creative journeys with intention, ultimately leading to a life rich with purpose, fulfillment, and connection.